# The
# Art
# Of Job
# Hunting

Myths, Secrets and Truths

**Willorna Brock**

**Published by**

Peaches

Publications

Published in London by Peaches Publications LTD, 2023.
www.peachespublications.co.uk

British Library Cataloguing in Publication Data: A catalogue record for this book is available from the British Library.

**ISBN:** 9798379225391

**Book cover design:** Peaches Publications LTD.
**Editor and Typesetter:** Linda Green.
**Proof-reader:** Virginia Rounding.

# Table of Contents

DEDICATION.............................................................. 1

ACKNOWLEDGEMENTS ........................................... 2

PREFACE................................................................. 4

INTRODUCTION....................................................... 6

STARTING THE JOURNEY ....................................... 11

  SELF-EVALUATION: FINDING YOUR 'WHY'.................... 11
  CAREER COACHING ................................................. 18
  HOW TO POSITION YOURSELF AND STAY AHEAD OF THE
  CURVE IN THE POST-PANDEMIC ERA............................ 21
  HOW AND WHERE TO SEARCH ................................... 29
  RETURNING TO THE JOB MARKET AFTER A BREAK ........... 37

MAKING YOUR APPLICATION................................ 40

  CURRICULUM VITAE (CV)......................................... 40

PREPARING FOR THE SELECTION PROCESS ........... 53

  SELECTION TESTS ................................................... 53

OTHER TYPES OF CANDIDATE ASSESSMENTS........ 54

INTERVIEWS .......................................................... 56

  DRESS CODE ......................................................... 58
  INTERVIEWS .......................................................... 60
  EXAMPLE JOB DESCRIPTION ...................................... 66

CORRESPONDING INTERVIEW QUESTIONS FOR JOB
DESCRIPTION ........................................................ 71

  MULTIPLE INTERVIEWS.............................................. 74
  QUESTIONS THE INTERVIEWER SHOULD NOT ASK YOU ..... 78

JOB OFFER AND ACCEPTANCE – HOW TO AVOID
BUYER'S REMORSE................................................. 82

PREPARING FOR YOUR NEW JOB .......................... 86

SELF-CARE – AVOIDING JOB-HUNTING BURNOUT 89

**EPILOGUE** ............................................................. **91**

**ABOUT THE AUTHOR** .......................................... **94**

**USEFUL LINKS** ..................................................... **97**

**APPENDICES** ........................................................ **98**

    APPENDIX 1: EXAMPLE CV ........................................ 98
    APPENDIX 2: EXAMPLE COVER LETTER ...................... 100
    APPENDIX 3: EXAMPLE OF SPECULATIVE EMAIL ........... 102
    APPENDIX 4: ADDITIONAL INTERVIEW QUESTIONS ....... 105
    APPENDIX 5: CAREER COACHING CASE STUDIES ........... 108

# Dedication

This book is dedicated to the memory of three unforgettable people in my life. My mother, Pearl Zuzella Luke (née Beckley), whom I lost as a teenager but I know is looking down on me, and to her parents, my grandparents Zuzel and Elme Beckley, with whom I spent my formative years.

My grandmother Elme was an Educationist to the core. She was awarded a British Empire Medal (BEM) for services to Education in colonial Sierra Leone. She instilled that love of learning and developing people in me.

# Acknowledgements

This is my second book on job hunting, the first having been published in August 2019.

God is first in everything I do, so I would like to thank my Heavenly Father for giving me courage, faith, strength, and many talents to continue this work.

Huge thanks to my family especially my three sons for their unconditional love and support.

The first edition of this book was self-published. This time around, I have had the support of Winsome Duncan and her awesome team. Winsome is a truly genuine spirit whose mission is to help others succeed. She has encouraged me to believe in myself and stop hiding! I feel blessed and grateful that our paths crossed.

Linda Green, my editor, has been my critical friend. I have thoroughly enjoyed our sessions. Thank you for your wisdom and sense of humour. Laughter is indeed a stressed author's medicine.

I wouldn't have met Winsome and her team without the recommendation of my ex-colleague, fellow teacher Miriam Manderson. Once a teacher, always a teacher. It is in our DNA to help people grow. Thank you, Miriam, for sharing your experience and tips.

Special thanks to my fellow career coach Anne Wilson, Head of Careers at the University of Warwick, England, who kindly agreed to share some of her insights.

Finally, a huge thank-you to all my career-coaching clients and colleagues and my network who continue to support my journey.

# Preface

Less than six months after my first book, *Job Hunting: Myths, Secrets and Truths*, our world experienced an unprecedented set of events that would change our lives forever. COVID-19 changed how we live and work.

This pandemic presented many challenges but offered some opportunities, including evolving new ways of living and working, some of which have benefited society and are here to stay.

It is unlikely that we will return to our previous ways of doing things, what is certain is the pandemic accelerated the digital revolution.

*Every challenge is an opportunity.*

This new way of doing things has presented us with some opportunities. For instance, there are now possibilities to work from anywhere in the world, which means we can apply for work and engage in the recruitment process online for jobs in our home countries and abroad.

I was a bit ahead of my time in my first book, where I included sections on preparing for virtual interviews and looking after your mental health whilst job hunting. These two areas came to the fore during the pandemic. The online recruitment process, especially when it comes to virtual interviews, is certainly different from the in-person experience, and this must not be overlooked.

I have included up-to-date hints and tips for job hunting in what many might see as challenging times.

You will also see quotes on some pages – these are mantras I live by, my own personal self-motivation quotes. These really work. Try memorising them yourself.

I am confident that, if you follow the hints and tips in the book, you will succeed in your job search.

Wishing you every success in your endeavours.

# Introduction

I have been job hunting since I was a teenager. I was about 14 years old.

My first job was part-time (6 hours on a Saturday), selling clothes at a fashion stall at Peckham Indoor Market in South London, England.

For that job, there was no application form, CV or interview. I walked up to a charming lady named Sadie and asked her if she needed help on the stall. She was somewhat impressed by my bravery, though reluctant at first, but saw how interested I was in her clothes, so she decided to give me a chance.

Since that first job at age 14, I have had all manner of jobs. They include cleaning; distributing free magazines outside London Underground stations; being a Beauty Consultant in department stores in London's West End; Project Finance in Banking, as an officer in UK government departments, such as the Forensic Science Service and the Department of Trade and Industry; teaching in schools; lecturing in colleges; tutoring; and now being a Human Resources Manager or Consultant.

In my lifetime, I must have applied for hundreds of jobs, received a similar number of rejections, and attended countless interviews.

What has always kept me going is my determination. There were, of course, times when I became pretty down and depressed about the whole process. I have burst into tears of frustration over my laptop.

I still managed to succeed and secure roles in good organisations and helped others apply for jobs and succeed at interviews throughout the process.

When I was teaching, I provided career advice to my students and helped them prepare for interviews. In the late 1990s, I became a mentor in the London Borough of Southwark Black Mentor Scheme and have been mentoring ever since. I currently mentor graduates with Graduate Mentor.

I also host employability skills workshops, and in 2018 I launched 'Fit for the future,' an event for parents and young people to engage in, dealing with parenting issues and getting ready for the world of work.

As an Enterprise Adviser, I volunteered with the Mayor of London's scheme to support schools with their career strategy to ensure all pupils have access to good quality careers education and are prepared for work.

My close family and friends always approach me for advice on their job search and have always encouraged me to take up career advising.

Working in Human Resources (HR), I am now on the 'other side.' My experience in HR has enhanced my knowledge and given me insight into the jungle that is job hunting.

As an HR professional, I support and advise through the entire recruitment process – from organisational design, development, job design, job descriptions and adverts, through to preparation selection criteria, shortlisting and interview questions, so I am well versed in the process.

My track record of recruitment in HR is sound. I always succeed in helping managers hire for difficult-to-fill positions. I refine the job description and ensure I am positioning for the right market.
Job hunting is a job in itself. It is a skill that needs time, patience and dedication to achieve results. People need support. I am constantly disappointed with the lack of affordable career guidance available. As always, the people who need it most don't have access to it. I believe that this sadly means that many are not reaching their full potential. I don't like to see talent go to waste. There is plenty of talent out there, but sadly people are losing out because they do not have the right information.

I truly believe that one of my purposes in life is to help people, and I get so excited when my clients ring me and share good news!

I have written this book to cover the entire job-hunting process, from starting your journey to your first 100 days in a new job. I have also included a chapter on self-care, which I believe is really important as the process can be stressful.

In the Appendices, I have included additional information such as CV templates, cover letters and career-coaching case studies.

I hope this book will provide you with some insight into the jungle that is job hunting. I will share with you some myths, secrets and truths. It will tackle the serious stuff, but I will keep it light-hearted because sometimes you have to laugh to maintain your sanity.

*London 2023.*

*Lack of clarity leads to poor decision-making.*

# Starting the journey

## Self-evaluation: Finding your 'Why'

# Truth

Before you start any journey, you need to know where you want to go.

Crucially, you need to know **why** you want to go there.

First, establish where you want to go and why you want to go there. Then you must work out how you will get there.

Three key questions:

1. Where are you now?
2. What do you need to get to your goal?
3. How can you start your journey?

It's the same for job hunting. Are you looking for just any job, or is this linked to your long-term career goals?

- Is it your first job?
- Is it a career move or progression?
- What do you want from this job?

You need to find out about this field or occupation,

the sector, and the qualifications and experience you need. You need to be honest with yourself and establish whether you are willing to put in the hard work or long hours needed to be successful in this job.

You can start planning your job search after answering all these questions. You will need to be honest and prepared to put in some work to achieve your goals.

For example, you may not have the qualifications and experience required for the job, so you must consider updating your skills.

There are many ways you can carry out self-analysis. As a first step, you can complete an in-depth self-review by performing your career SWOT analysis. Below I describe a SWOT analysis:

S Strengths
W Weaknesses
O Opportunities
T Threats

When done thoroughly, the SWOT analysis is excellent because it allows you to think deeply, helping you to reveal things that you may not have considered about yourself. You can capture information about your strengths, weaknesses, opportunities, and threats. By understanding your weaknesses, for example, you will have identified gaps in knowledge, skills and behaviours (competencies) that you need to work on to become the best candidate for your target job.

You would undertake a SWOT analysis based on the requirements of the job or occupation you are interested in pursuing. Any requirements you don't currently have will provide you with the details of your knowledge gap. Think about it also as a 'gap analysis.' The SWOT analysis, therefore, puts you in the centre, helping you develop your talents, and enabling you to stand out against the competition in the job-hunting jungle.

**Strengths**
To help you understand your strengths, think of yourself as a product. Your own 'brand'.
A strength is an asset. It will make you stand out and can be used to your advantage by any future employer. When thinking about your strengths, you may wish to think of what other people or your line manager have identified as your strength.

Examples:

- Your education, knowledge, and experience
- Skills such as languages or project management
- Your network

**Weaknesses**
A weakness is something you are not very good at

or lack confidence doing. Weaknesses should be seen as areas for development. Try to be as objective as possible but don't be too hard on yourself. You could try to improve in this area to increase your chances of success in your job hunt.

Examples:

- Poor time management skills
- Needing to improve project management skills
- Being weak at Microsoft Excel

Consider things that you avoid doing because you lack confidence.

What negative traits do you sometimes display, and how can you work to improve them? For instance, do you struggle to arrive at work on time? Are you a poor listener? Are you afraid of speaking in front of an audience/presenting?

**Opportunities**

Opportunities are things from which you could benefit.

Examples

- Who in your network can help you?
- Are there any emerging trends in your industry?
- How can you take advantage of them?
- What new courses can you take to enhance your knowledge?

**Threats**

Threats are obstacles beyond your control that can affect your career goals. You will need to think about these carefully and find ways to address them. Examples

- What is the competition for the job for which you are applying?
- Are there issues in your personal life that could affect your success in this career, and how can you mitigate these?
- Are there any new or emerging technologies? For example, does the rise of artificial intelligence (AI) and robotics mean that your skills may no longer be required? It may present an opportunity, meaning you can change direction and acquire new skills.
- Are any weaknesses so severe that they could lead to threats?

Always remember that the personal SWOT analysis will help you home in on your strengths, improve on your weaknesses, identify opportunities for development and help you either minimise or overcome your threats.

**Useful questionnaires to help you discover yourself**

Apart from the SWOT analysis to assess your strengths, you can also use a range of questionnaires which can help you further. A colleague of mine listed them on her blog and has kindly agreed for me to include them for information. https://thecareercatalyst.co.uk/5-of-the-best-free-careers-questionnaires/

I have listed a few of them below and provided an introduction for each one. They are all free and easy to use.

Your motivations

Motivation is quite powerful. It is essentially what drives us. Understanding your motivations helps you to find your 'Why'. The Work Values Test helps you identify the type of work or career you prefer. https://www.123test.com/work-values-test/

Your preferences

This test gives you insight into your personality preferences. We are all made up of different psychological personality traits. You might find some people easier to get along with than others. Knowing all the different personality types and your own will empower you and help you handle your relationships, not just at work but also in life.

The 16 Personality Types profile is a great personality questionnaire to complete.

https://www.16personalities.com

Your strengths

The strengths test is useful if you struggle to identify your strengths. This test can help you discover quite a lot about yourself. Not only will you learn about your strengths, but you will also uncover strengths of which you may not be aware.
https://www.strengthsprofile.com/en-GB/Products/Free

Your values

Knowing your true values and what you believe in helps you decide the type of work you would like to do and the type of organisation for which you would like to work. These days, organisations place a lot of emphasis on their values, which you can usually find on their website.

Organisations like to employ people whose values align with theirs. The personal values assessment https://www.valuescentre.com/tools-assessments/pva/ is a simple survey that takes just a few minutes of your time and provides a wealth of information about why you do what you do.

Self-awareness is important. Knowing who you are, what you stand for, and your strengths and weaknesses is a key factor in success, not just in your career. Self-awareness sets the pace for the best version of yourself.

Job seekers who are self-aware and know what transferable skills they have to offer are much more likely to succeed than those with no plans at all.

## Career Coaching

Finally, if you are struggling with choices or are at a loss about which direction to take, you can invest in career coaching sessions. If you are at college or university, you can access this through your University Careers Service. Some organisations provide this for free or at a low cost, and I provide career coaching as part of my service.

For an idea of how career coaching works, I have included some case studies in Appendix 5.

## Secret

By doing your SWOT analysis or completing any of the questionnaires I have listed above, you will learn much about yourself and become more self-aware, which will help you prepare for interviews.

I am sure you have heard about interview questions which ask you about your strengths and weaknesses. Nevertheless, you will not discuss weaknesses in an interview.

If you struggle to identify your strengths and weaknesses, why don't you look at the job description for your ideal job? Look at the competencies you need for that job and take it from there.

# Myth

Other people can appear perfect. No one is perfect. We all have our weaknesses. What is important is self-awareness, trying to be the best we can be to overcome our weaknesses.

*It is what it is. Let go of the past and move on.*

## How to position yourself and stay ahead of the curve in the post-pandemic era

If you are not growing, you are dying.

I firmly believe in lifelong learning and always say that I will be learning until I take my last breath. As long as you have breath, you learn and grow every day. It doesn't mean having to study for demanding qualifications. It doesn't mean reading all the time extensively, just the little things. Being curious and asking lots of questions.

There is always something to be learned from every experience in life, good or bad.

To be successful in your career, you need to learn and grow, which will benefit you in terms of career or job success and is also good for your well-being and sense of worth. Focusing on growth and positivity helps remove your mind from negative issues and gives you a sense of purpose.

COVID-19 changed the world forever. Now more than ever, you must remain ahead of the curve in a fast-changing world. By this statement, I mean that it is essential to focus on your personal development and keep your skills up to date.

You should try to engage in a range of activities to be successful not just in getting the job but also once in the job. It doesn't end when you receive that job offer. To succeed and stay ahead of the game, you must embrace continuous development and a lifelong learning mindset.

Staying ahead of the game is how you will gain recognition at work, get promoted and obtain skills that will set you up for a successful career.

Top skills demanded by employers

The World Economic Forum Future of Jobs Report 2020[1] lists the top skills needed in the future of work.

It is worth bearing these skills in mind during job hunting and as part of your continuous personal development and lifelong learning goals.

- Analytical thinking
- Active learning and learning strategies
- Complex problem solving
- Critical thinking and analysis
- Creativity, originality and initiative
- Leadership and social influence
- Technology use, monitoring and control

---

[1] World Economic Forum (20 October 2020) 'The Future of Jobs Report 2020', accessed on 26.10.2022 at: https://www.weforum.org/reports/the-future-of-jobs-report-2020/in-full/infographics-e4e69e4de7

- Technology design and programming
- Resilience, stress tolerance and flexibility
- Reasoning, problem solving and innovation

<u>Your personal record of achievements</u>

When you are busy at work, it is easy to get so engrossed in it that you forget the things you are doing and the value you are adding to your employer. A good way around this is to record your achievements. Find time, make it a priority or schedule time in your diary to reflect on things you are doing at work, projects you are working on, and the results you are achieving.

I always say, "Document your successes and your failures."

Remember that failures are lessons learned. Note down your thoughts about things you do.

**WWW** – What went well? What was really good about this piece of work? How were you able to be successful in the delivery of this piece of work?

**EBI** – Even better if …? What were some of the challenges you encountered? What could you have done better?

This technique will also help when you come to do interviews because you are likely to be asked questions about successes and failures at work. We will delve deeper into this when we talk about interviews.

<u>Coaching and mentoring</u>

I strongly believe that everyone would benefit from having a coach or a mentor at some point in their career. Some organisations have coaching and mentoring programmes to help employees to learn and grow. Many leadership programmes involve coaching and mentoring.

According to the Chartered Institute of Personnel and Development (CIPD), the United Kingdom's leading professional organisation for Human Resources (HR) and Learning and Development (L&D), coaching and mentoring are development approaches based on the use of one-to-one conversations to enhance an individual's skills, knowledge or work performance. It's possible to draw distinctions between coaching and mentoring, although, in practice, the terms are often used interchangeably.

**What is coaching?**

Coaching aims to produce specific performance and improvement goals. It usually involves you working with someone who will guide you to achieve your goals. A coach will not directly tell you what to do but will work with you as an accountability partner.

Mentoring is slightly different as it involves working with someone who is more experienced than you. They are usually a more senior person in your field or your line of work who has been through your journey and will be there to offer advice and guidance.

Having a coach or a mentor helps to propel your career as they will act as a sounding board. You can develop a good relationship, and that person can help you build your network.

To summarise:

A coach *coaches* you to help you achieve your goals
A mentor *shares their experience* with you to help you achieve your goals

**Your brand**
Your brand is your online digital presence.

- What do you stand for?
- What are your passions?
- What are your strengths?
- Which platforms do you use?
- Who do you follow?

All of the above forms a perception of you to your future employer.

I mention brand because you can use this to position yourself and stay ahead of the curve with your online activity. If you position yourself very well, for example, on LinkedIn, you are likely to be approached by employers, so they do the chasing, and you don't.

I will discuss the importance of your LinkedIn profile in detail later.

# Truth

Did you know that employers check your online profile?

Some employers now carry out social media checks as part of pre-employment background screening.

The guide below is from Experian, a leading credit and reference checking agency, sharing information about social media screening.

https://www.experian.co.uk/blogs/latest-thinking/background-checks/social-media-checks-what-are-they-and-why-are-they-important/

**Finally, I share ten top tips for a post-pandemic world:**

1.  Change is constant – be ahead of the curve

2.  Have a good understanding of your working environment at a macro and micro level – understand the forces at play

3.  Constantly self-assess and develop yourself – sharpen your axe

4.  Have a growth and positive mindset – think outside the box

5.  Build your professional network – be strategic and intentional

6.  Develop your online presence – be visible

7.  Keep a 'Success Journal' – your achievements are key

8.  Have a mentor - for accountability and direction

9.  Keep your CV up to date - review every six months

10. Take care of your health and well-being

*Where there is life,*
*there is hope.*

## How and where to search

It's incredible to think that, just a few years ago, one would only look for jobs in the newspapers or go and meet with agencies. The COVID-19 pandemic accelerated the move to all things digital, so almost everything is online.

<u>List of places to search</u>

These places include but are not limited to:

- Industry magazines
- Job fairs (including virtual)
- Jobsites – Indeed, CV-Library, Reed
- Networking sites – online groups, WhatsApp groups, LinkedIn and Facebook groups
- Newspapers
- Recruitment agencies
- Social media platforms – LinkedIn, Facebook, Instagram, Twitter

**Visibility – getting yourself out there**

**Networking**
Your network is your net worth. There is a 'hidden jobs' market, meaning about 70–80% of jobs are not advertised. Therefore, it is important to network, get to know people, attend seminars and online webinars, join professional groups and widen your

circle. Networking has become huge and many people get jobs through their networks. I will talk more about networking under 'How and where to search'.

Networking means that you need to craft your brand. A strong personal brand means you build and establish relationships, which helps you connect with companies and people hiring.

Therefore, getting involved in networking groups, letting your friends and family know that you are looking, and reaching out to recruiters and hiring managers are tried and tested ways to secure the bag.

I was 19 when I reached out directly to a company and wrote my first speculative letter. I worked at Midland Bank (now HSBC) and wanted to work in international banking. I wrote a letter to National Westminster (Natwest) Bank's Head Office about my interest. I was invited to interview and received an offer to work in their Energy and Natural resources team, within Corporate Finance. This was based at the NatWest Tower in the City of London, which is now the 'Tower 42' building.

**Recruitment agencies**

Recruitment agencies are also a good source for roles.

A word of caution about some recruitment agencies (UK). Some do not deliver a good candidate experience. They will inform you that they will put you forward for jobs, and you won't hear from them again. I used to get upset about this and took it personally. It is certainly not good for your mental well-being when you're desperately seeking a job, but just be reassured that it's not only you. They do that with everyone. I know of very senior, highly experienced professionals who complain about this. So don't take it personally, and don't put up with bad treatment. Find an agency that works for you and move on. Good agencies will devote time to you and look after you very well.

I had a much better candidate experience when I went directly to an employer rather than through an agency.

See Appendix 3 for an example of a speculative application email.

## Using a systematic approach for your job search

Job hunting is a job in itself. If you are serious about securing your dream role, you must be committed to doing it properly to achieve the desired results. By being committed, I mean being organised, having a routine, setting time to do your research, completing job applications, preparing for interviews and reflecting on interviews or conversations you have had with potential employers. I would suggest having a spreadsheet with a list of recruiters and a list of jobs you have applied for and interviewed for, with notes to help you remember important details.

# Truth

Job hunting can be a very stressful experience, especially if you are under financial pressure. Try to maintain a positive mindset at all times. There is always light at the end of the tunnel. Be kind to yourself.

- Take time out and switch off when it gets too much
- Pray or meditate
- Spend time with loved ones
- Listen to music
- Do something that makes you laugh or smile

# Secret

A lot of jobs now are advertised by sector. Some websites and agencies specialise in specific fields only. Why not try and find out who they are and where the employers you are interested in advertise their vacancies?

**Changing career**

Sometimes we start to feel unhappy about work. We find that our job is no longer fulfilling. We know deep down that things are not right. Life is too short to be unhappy at work. Realistically it is not always possible financially to throw in the towel immediately and give up a job with which we have fallen out of love. However, some steps can be taken to achieve a new career goal. Proper planning and patience are needed. For this, it is back to self-awareness and self-evaluation. Make sure you do your homework. Find out about the job, the sector, how much it pays, and the opportunities for career development. Most importantly, you need to check what qualifications you need. You can check online job adverts to determine the required skills and qualifications. To invest time and money into studying for a new qualification, you must do your research thoroughly.

**Life after redundancy**

At the time of writing this edition (November 2022), the world is going through unprecedented economic uncertainty, with many countries facing high inflation, high interest rates and talk of a recession. There was a time when it was difficult to talk about redundancy; people felt it was their fault and wondered how they would come across to you employees.

Some people lost their jobs during the pandemic. Now many people are facing redundancy. All too often, people who have been made redundant immediately look to find a similar job elsewhere; this is understandable as there are bills to pay.

Suppose you have been made redundant and managed to secure a decent redundancy or severance package, which means you can afford to take a few weeks off. Why not take a step back and use this as an opportunity to consider whether the job you were in before is really what you want?
Resist the temptation to spend that money on an exotic trip or a new kitchen. Treat yourself by all means, but how about spending money on training and development for a new career?

If you are unclear about which direction to take, spend time on self-evaluation. Please bear in mind that career change may require patience and some sacrifices. I know I had to do this when I moved from teaching to HR.

As a career changer, you may have reached a senior level in your previous occupation and expect to remain at the same level. Unfortunately, it doesn't always work that way (you may be one of the lucky ones), but it takes years of experience, not just education and qualifications, to get to the top of most professions. You need to earn your stripes. So be prepared to start in a more junior role and work your way up. If you are dedicated and smart, work hard and use your transferable skills, you will impress, and it won't take long to move up anyway.

# Secret

When I moved from teaching to Human Resources (HR), I had about six years of teaching experience, helping to run my school's language department, but when I started in HR, I started as an HR Assistant. I started in a non-paid role, but after six months, I was offered a paid position as a temp via an agency and subsequently secured a permanent position at the organisation. Within three years, I secured an HR Officer role with a Big 4 firm.

Don't ever be put off by having to start again. It is better than staying in a job or field where you are unhappy. Time flies, and before you know it, you will have moved up in your new career and be living your best life! It is possible to go two steps back and ten steps forward!

*Embrace*
*change*
*with vigour.*

**Returning to the job market after a break**

The thought of returning to work after a break can be daunting. If this is after a period of redundancy, thankfully everyone knows the effect COVID-19 had on the job market, so if you are one of those who were made redundant, it shouldn't be too difficult to explain your employment gap. One silver lining of the pandemic was people showing empathy and being human, something I have always advocated.

The key to making a successful return to the workplace is capitalising on your transferable skills. So, if you are asked to explain your employment gap, be honest, and talk about what you have done during that time to improve yourself, skills you have gained, voluntary work experience you did, and talk about your transferable skills.

List all your transferable skills if you took time off to care for children or elderly relatives. During your time off, you managed a multi-tasked home. You may have done some voluntary work and have previous work experience, all of which are attractive to a potential employer. What did you do if you took the time to travel around the world? What new skills did you learn? How have you grown as a person? All of these are valuable skills to sell. What matters is how you position yourself.

You have transferable skills if you previously took time off to travel or pursue personal projects. Employers like people who can think outside the box and have more to bring to the table. See the list of the top skills demanded by employers on page 20.

Many employers are now offering 'Returnships' too. Why not look into this option?

## Secret

You can limit gaps in your CV by doing some voluntary work. That shows that you have remained active and engaged in meaningful work, adding value whilst acquiring new skills.

*You are enough.*

## Making your application

# Truth

You have seen the role you want to apply for, and you will need a Curriculum Vitae (CV) to make your application. It is also referred to as a 'resume', especially in the United States of America (USA).

You may need to upload this to an online application portal, or you may need to send it to a recruiter by email.

Keep track of what you do so your CV updates are easy.

### Curriculum Vitae (CV)

What is a CV?

A CV summarises your life in terms of your education and work record.

Your CV is usually the first thing a recruiter or a hiring manager sees about you, so I cannot stress enough how important this document is.

A recruiter or a hiring manager will only spend a few seconds (less than 15) looking at your CV initially.

They might spend less time if they are inundated with hundreds of CVs. Recruiters and hiring managers look for keywords related to the job description. The CV needs to interest them enough to want to speak with you in more detail to find out more.

We live in a very competitive world. Living in the digital age means that not just humans will see your CV first. With the rise of artificial intelligence (AI), machines are also programmed to scan CVs. The volume of applications means that companies need help scanning CVs. These machines (or the software used to operate them) are called applicant tracking systems (ATS).

The key is to ensure that your CV gets you an interview. Whilst writing this book, a friend sent me his CV to review for him. I first noticed its length, sheer wordiness, long paragraphs, stories, and explanations. He could have presented the information succinctly in bullet points instead.

If I were a recruiter or a hiring manager with lots of CVs to look at, I would not skim through all that information.
ATS software reads your CV within 2 to 6 seconds. If your CV is not ATS-friendly, it will be rejected. ATS look for keywords in the job description, so ensure that these are reflected in your CV.

Your CV needs to be succinct and no more than two pages. For some jobs, especially senior academic positions, where people have had lots of experience and written papers, more than two pages may be OK, but generally, a maximum of two pages.

<u>How to beat ATS software</u>

- Tailor your CV to the job description each time you apply for a job
- Make sure that you include keywords from the job description on your CV or cover letter
- Avoid abbreviations and use the full description of the course, e.g., Master of Business Administration (MBA)
- Do not use tables or columns on your CV, as this usually causes your CV to be rejected in an automated selection process
- Use standard CV fonts such as Arial, Calibri, Cambria, Helvetica or Tahoma
- Use a font size no bigger than 12 for the main body and no bigger than 16 for your name

# Truth

Your CV needs to generate enough interest for the employer to want to meet with you to find out more about you before deciding whether to interview you. A CV is what will get you through the door.

What do you need in a CV?

The content in your CV should reflect what the employer is looking for in a potential employee. It needs to demonstrate that you have the competencies required for the job.

What are competencies?

Competencies are knowledge, skills and behaviours that are relevant to the job. They are usually displayed in the job description.

Your CV needs to show that you have these competencies, making you a potential candidate so that they will want to find out more about you and call you in for an interview.

Your CV will usually demonstrate your knowledge and skills, and your interview will test your knowledge and skills AND your behaviours.

What should be included in a CV?

Basic information:

• Profile or Professional summary – this is a brief introduction about you. It should not be your entire life history but something to attract interest.
• Key skills and achievements – this is useful to talk about things you have done in the past that have added value – e.g., skills and achievements in the job description.

- Experience or Career history – this should be written in reverse chronological order. Put your current job at the top. For each job, write the name of the company and a brief line about what you did and your role. You don't need to write the full address of the company, e.g., JCB PLC, Birmingham or, if in a different country, e.g., CGI Inc, Washington, USA.
- Dates should be in a consistent format throughout the CV, e.g.:
  Jan 2020 – Date
  Feb 2021 – Aug 2022 not in one paragraph 01/2020 for the date, and in another paragraph Feb 2021 – August 2022
- Education / Qualifications
- Awards / Voluntary work – only if relevant to the job you are applying for.

**What you must have in your CV**

- Good quality of layout
- Competencies relevant to the role
- Positive action words

**What you should avoid in your CV**

- Spelling mistakes
- Overly elaborate formatting
- Irrelevant information

# Secret

Always have a 'base CV' with all your key skills and experience. Adjust your CV with keywords from the job description of each job application.

Please see Appendix 1 for an example CV.

# Myth

'Young people at school or people with little work experience can't have a CV', or 'It is difficult to have a CV if you have been out of work for a while.'

# Truth

Young people can have a CV. People who have been out of work can have a CV.

When I have been asked to help a young person find work experience, my first question is always – Do they have a CV? I always get a bemused response followed by laughter.

Most people have transferable skills, i.e., skills they may not have gained at work, which can be transferred into the workplace.

If you are a school leaver or a recent graduate

without formal work experience, you can include relevant activities you have engaged in that are related to the job.
Examples:

• Club or group leader
• Organiser
• Duke of Edinburgh Awards (UK)

Young people have many transferable skills from school or extra-curricular activities that can be used in the workplace.

Similarly, stay-at-home mothers will have developed skills such as time management, financial management – for instance, handling family finances, – and they may have volunteered on the Parent Teacher Association (PTA), etc. These experiences can be outlined on a CV to show the employer that the candidate has valuable transferable skills.

## Cover letters

Including a cover letter with your CV when applying for a job is good practice. A carefully written cover letter will allow you to introduce yourself further to a potential employer, and you can expand on your relevant skills for the job.

The cover letter is what the name implies. You are sending your CV and attaching a letter to introduce yourself, saying why you are applying and are a good candidate for the job.

Your cover letter should highlight and refer to your competencies for the job listed in your CV. You are saying, 'This is me. Here is my CV. I have the skills you want, and you can see all this in my CV.' You will also use this opportunity to elaborate on what's in your CV, using examples from your work experience.

Please see Appendix 2 for an example of a cover letter.

# Secret

Always put effort into preparing your application for a job. Take your time to prepare your CV and cover letter. Ensure you have read the job description very well and tailored your CV for the job you are applying for. Employers can distinguish candidates who have invested much time and effort in their application from those who haven't. If they get the impression that you haven't, it demonstrates that you don't care much about working for them and are just applying to them because any job will do.

Print all documents and proofread them before sending them. I usually 'sleep on my applications' , meaning I don't work on them and send them off the same day.

I go to bed and wake up the following morning and look at them again with a 'fresh pair of eyes.'

When you are tired or have been staring at a document for a long time, you will not see errors on the screen.

Don't omit to check details like spelling, etc. Typos are a no-no. Employers frown on incorrect spelling and grammatical errors. Don't allow a typo to get in the way of you and your dream job!

I mentioned the importance of your 'brand' earlier. Social media can be powerful if used the right way.

**LinkedIn** is the most popular network for professionals. I have met and formed many valuable and rewarding professional connections on LinkedIn. I have also been headhunted for jobs on LinkedIn.

I can attest to the power of a good LinkedIn profile that engages with the right connections. As we know, the pandemic accelerated the move to online and the virtual world of work. During the pandemic, I met many people on LinkedIn, which was one of my key places to network, engage and learn.

The power of a professional LinkedIn profile cannot be overstated, particularly when trying to network with others, gain new job opportunities or increase your profile in your field.

A good LinkedIn profile will help you gain visibility, allowing you to position yourself and stay ahead of the curve, as I mentioned in Chapter 1.

A strong profile will:

- Attract interest from recruiters – they will come to you

- Enable you to network with like-minded professionals, so you learn valuable skills as well as knowledge about your field or sector; this will help you in your job applications and interviews

- Build your reputation as a professional

It doesn't take much to improve your LinkedIn profile. You can do this yourself as there are many guides on the LinkedIn site and online that you can access too.Below are some quick wins you can leverage to improve your LinkedIn profile page.

**Your photo**

First impressions count. Whilst you don't need a perfect picture, you do need a photo that is decent enough for people to take you seriously.

**Your headline**

Your headline is the most essential aspect of your LinkedIn profile.

Think of it as your unique selling point (USP). You must have heard of USP before. Again, this is something I have mentioned before – 'your brand'.

Your headline makes you stand out as a professional, summed up in one short sentence. It is just below your name and is designed to attract other LinkedIn users and encourage them to connect with you, building the professional relationships that will support your career.

Your headline summarises who you are and what you want from your career.

Keep it short, be honest about your strengths and promote yourself.

**Your summary**

The 'About' section is a summary of you. People viewing your profile, including recruiters, will see this, so try to craft this so that people will want to engage with you.

In your summary, discuss yourself, sharing your background, successes, and career objectives. You should also ensure that this demonstrates your value add to an employer.

**Your connections**

Be careful about the company you keep. The people you engage with on LinkedIn demonstrate to others your likes, your values and what you stand for.

Who you follow and engage with on social media platforms indicates the kind of person you are.

If you are trying to learn and grow your career, you should follow and learn from leaders in your field.

A key benefit of LinkedIn is the ability to build relationships with relevant professionals in your field. Make sure that your connections are those who can add value to your professional development. With this in mind, it is worth thinking carefully about the connection requests you accept.

Doing this ensures that you build relationships with relevant professionals in your field. It also saves time as you gain a more meaningful experience from the platform instead of your feed being full of irrelevant information or marketing material.

**Experience, Education, Licences and Certifications, Volunteering and Skills**

These sections are self-explanatory. It is worth ensuring they are similar to what you have included in your CV because prospective employers will likely check your LinkedIn profile. You can also add the qualifications that you are currently studying for.

**Recommendations**

Recommendations are LinkedIn's version of testimonials. You can ask current and former colleagues, teachers, or lecturers to comment on your professional skills, experience, and knowledge. Anyone you are connected with on LinkedIn can give you a recommendation.

These recommendations provide insight into who you are and are useful for improving your brand and visibility.

**Your background cover image**

Your cover image sits behind your profile picture at the top of your page.

LinkedIn has a default background cover image, but you can create one unique to you and the image you would like to project.

A simple photo, quote, or phrase are good examples of what you can have as your background cover image.

You can create one by using a graphics platform like Canva.

By working on the appearance of your LinkedIn profile, you will present a good impression of your professional brand. It will help if you are job hunting or want to grow your network and connect with like-minded people. Preparing for the selection process

## Selection tests

You will sometimes be asked to undertake a pre-selection test before your interview. If carried out before your interview, this allows the employer to carry out the initial sift. These tests include psychometric and aptitude tests. Most employers will inform you beforehand, and many will indicate what type of test you will take. If they don't tell you, please ask. You should be provided with information about the test you will be undertaking. I advise you to allow plenty of time to practise and prepare before taking the final tests. There are plenty of sample tests available online.

# Other types of candidate assessments

There are various types of candidate assessments. You may be required to participate in one or more of the following:

- Completing written exercises

- Delivering a presentation

- Group activities

- Roleplays

Always seek as much information as you can and prepare adequately.

*Failures are lessons learned.*
*I am a work in progress.*

# Interviews

### Interview preparation

It is usual to have a mix of telephone, video and in-person interviews. For some jobs, a telephone or video interview is likely to take place during the initial stages of the selection process, and then you may be asked to attend in person to meet your prospective employer during the final stage.

As part of the initial screening, telephone and video interviews allow your potential employer to find out enough about you to decide whether to take you to the next stage of the interview process.

For all interviews, regardless of the format, preparation is key.

For telephone interviews and video interviews, get yourself into interview mode. Take the phone call or have your video interview in a quiet place where you will not have any distractions. What you wear will impact your performance. Dress as you would if you were attending in person.

If you are in your pyjamas or your home clothes when doing these types of interviews, you are unlikely to behave in the same manner as you would if you were washed, fed, watered and dressed up for a face-to-face interview.

**Tips for telephone and video interviews:**

1. Check your camera, audio settings, background and lighting before the interview. If the lighting is poor, invest in a decent video conference lighting kit. It doesn't need to be very expensive.
2. Position your laptop so you can be seen properly by the interviewer(s).
3. Get dressed, and sit in a room, preferably with a desk, away from all distractions such as the postman, pets, children and noisy people in the household.
4. Have a copy of your CV, application and interview notes and the job description with you.
5. Ensure that your phone is fully charged.
6. You should be expecting their call, so answer your phone in a professional manner.

For example, you would say good morning or afternoon, this is YOUR FULL NAME.

7. Remain calm and confident.
8. Speak slowly and ask any questions you don't understand to be repeated.
9. Ensure you impress so you can be invited for a face-to-face interview.
10. At the end of the interview, say thank you and that you look forward to hearing from them.

**Dress code**

In thinking about the dress code, what type of organisation is it in terms of culture? Always go for the culture. If it's a traditional organisation, like government, law firms or professional services, keep it formal.

If it is a start-up in the creative or technology space, you can go for a business casual look.

If you are in doubt, you can check their website, LinkedIn page, and social media channels such as YouTube or Instagram to get a feel for their culture. It is better to dress in formal attire than to wear casual clothes.

# Myth

Being nervous is a bad thing.

# Secret

*Timing*

Wherever possible, arrange your interviews at a time that suits you, when you are likely to perform at your best. If you are not a morning person, avoid 9.00 a.m. interviews if possible.

If you are attending in person, allow yourself plenty of time to get there. It is best to arrive early so you can relax and gather your thoughts before the interview.

When you arrive, be friendly and polite.

*Approach*

When you arrive at your face-to-face interview, be friendly and pleasant to everyone you come across. Be friendly with the receptionist or the person who escorts you to the interview room. Do not underestimate the power of these people. A negative comment about your attitude to them can turn off your prospective employer because it will say a lot about you.

*Nerves*

Be yourself.
Don't worry if you don't meet all the job requirements.
If they like you, your strengths are strong, and the employer feels they can live with your weaknesses, e.g., if someone in the team can fill the gaps, they will take you on.

What matters is your enthusiasm, passion, humility and willingness to learn.

# Truth

To be nervous is human. The interviewer is human. If you are a bit nervous, they will see that you are keen. Being overly confident is not always good. You may come across as arrogant and potentially difficult in the workplace. The person interviewing you might be having a bad day. They might be so busy and could do without interviewing you. They might have been called in to step in for their colleague who should have been interviewing you. So don't take things personally. Smile and be calm.

**Interviews**

You may have one or more people interviewing you as part of a panel.

The interview will usually start with greetings, introductions and a general conversation, 'small talk' to break the ice and make you feel comfortable. If it's a face-to-face interview, small talk will include random things like the weather (if you are in the UK), your journey there, how easily you found the location, etc. If it's a video interview, it is likely to be informal questions about yourself. Don't go into too much detail or talk too much. Be natural and friendly.

You will then be asked questions about your

professional history, education, and why you want the job. They will also ask about your competencies for the job and what you know about the company.

Most of the questions relate to the job description. The interviewer(s) want to determine whether your skills, knowledge and behaviours are relevant for the job. They want to find out whether you are a good fit for the role and whether they would enjoy working with you.

# Truth

The interview is not just about whether you can do the job. It is also to see whether you would be a valuable team member. Likeability is a factor here too.

**How to structure your response to interview questions**

How you respond to interview questions is the deal maker or breaker.

A typical interview starter question is: 'Tell me about yourself' or 'Talk me through your CV.'

Most interviewers will ask you *competency-based* questions.
These questions ask you to provide real-life

examples from your previous work or voluntary experience of how you acted or responded to specific scenarios. They are designed so that you can demonstrate your knowledge, skills, and behaviours required for the job in your answer. The best way to handle competency-based questions is to provide your answers in a structured manner, like telling a story, using the 'STAR' or 'CAR' approach. This approach helps to avoid 'waffling' – talking too much, providing too much irrelevant information or going off tangent in your answer. Waffling can happen in an interview scenario when you feel nervous. We have all been there. I have been in interview panels where I have seen very experienced, and senior, people make this mistake.

To avoid waffling, it is better to follow one of these formats.

I have set out below an outline of the 'STAR' and 'CAR' approaches. Both are similar, and you can choose which one you find easier.

> **S**ituation – set the scene. Describe the situation or scenario so that the interviewer gets the picture and understands your example.

> **T**ask – share what your responsibility was and what you were trying to achieve from the situation or scenario.

Action – explain how you addressed or resolved the situation or scenario.

Result – highlight the outcome, what you achieved and any learnings you took away from it.

The CAR approach is a shorter version of the STAR approach. Some people find it easier to use to structure their answers.

Context or Challenge – set the scene. Describe what the situation or scenario was so that the interviewer gets the picture and understands your example.

Action – share your responsibility and what you tried to achieve from the situation or scenario. What did you do to resolve it?

Result – highlight the outcome, what you achieved and any learnings you took away from it.

Focus on what *you* did and avoid using 'we'. Remember that the interviewer knows nothing about this situation or scenario. Take your time and explain the steps and the sequence of events.

### The 'STAR' approach: Example question for an HR interview

*'Tell me about a time you resolved a business problem.'*

Situation: We had a problem with lots of people leaving. We were unable to retain people. As a result, we were spending a lot of money on recruitment. Our turnover rate was 50% per year.

Task: I decided to find out why this was happening so that we could reduce the staff turnover rate.
Action: I conducted some surveys to find out why people were leaving. I also interviewed current staff to find out what they liked/disliked about working in the company.

Result: The surveys and interviews gave us valuable insight into staff satisfaction, and we identified the issues. People were unhappy and disengaged. I worked with the team to put in place strategies to improve staff engagement, and after a year, attrition was reduced by half to 25%. As a result, we reduced our recruitment costs by 50%.

Below is the 'CAR' approach for the same question, but this time, you are condensing your answer into three sections instead of four.

*Challenge:* We had a problem with lots of people leaving. We were unable to retain people. As a result, we were spending a lot of money on recruitment. Our turnover rate was 50% per year.

*Action:* I decided to find out why this was happening so that we could reduce the staff turnover rate. I carried out some surveys to find out why people were leaving. I also interviewed current staff to find out what they liked/disliked about working in the company.

*Result:* The surveys and interviews gave us valuable insight into staff satisfaction, and we identified the issues. People were unhappy and disengaged. I worked with the team to put in place strategies to improve staff engagement, and after a year, attrition was reduced by half to 25%. As a result, we reduced our recruitment costs by 50%.

When responding to interview questions, remember the 'two-minute rule.' Try not to speak longer than two minutes. Keep your answers concise. If they want to know more, they will ask. The idea is to provide key facts that will arouse their interest and make them probe further.

In all your responses, be honest. If you don't know the answer or haven't done a particular thing before, say so. Say you don't know, but you are willing to learn.

## Examples of interview questions based on a job description

As part of your interview preparation, it is worth looking at the job description to understand what the role entails and what skills, knowledge and behaviours (competencies) you need to demonstrate at the interview. Good interview preparation means preparing to answer possible questions.

I have provided below a job description and related interview questions. Have a good look at both items to understand how interview questions come about.

**Example job description**

Executive Assistant (EA) to the Director of Finance at Sierra Capital Investors

To provide comprehensive administrative support to the Director of Project Finance, responsible for diary management, handling complex travel itineraries through liaison with internal and external stakeholders and supporting with ad-hoc project work.

Key areas of responsibility:

- Diary management

- Manage complex travel arrangements, including itineraries, flights, hotels, transfers and visas as necessary
- Manage the Director's correspondence, including mail and email, proactively (prioritising where appropriate)

- Act as point of contact, ensuring that all telephone calls, posts and queries are responded to promptly, appropriately and professionally

- Plan and coordinate internal and external meetings as required, ensuring all presentations, briefings, documents, and minutes are prepared and follow-up actions are progressed as appropriate

- Produce correspondence and documents, some of which may be of a sensitive or highly confidential nature

- Develop and maintain excellent working relationships with a range of internal and external contacts at all levels of seniority

- Assist with projects, working to tight deadlines

- Undertake research and analysis to support the Director and his team

- Events management, working closely with the Projects team

- Manage the Director's expenses and timesheets

- Undertake ad-hoc administrative duties as required

Competencies required

- Good standard of education and relevant professional experience

- Extensive experience working as an Executive Assistant for C-Suite or senior management

- Highly organised and efficient, with the ability to anticipate needs and prioritise tasks and coordinate projects under pressure of deadlines

- Ability to manage electronic diaries, coordinate appointments (internal and external) and ensure all necessary arrangements are in place

- Excellent relationship-building and interpersonal skills with the ability to deal with a variety of people at different levels

- Ability to convey complex information clearly and concisely, including taking accurate notes and action lists at meetings

- Excellent written and oral communication skills, including addressing a wide range of audiences and sensitivity to different cultural contexts

- Excellent attention to detail

- Proficiency in the use of Microsoft Office and aptitude for learning and using a variety of software packages

- Ability to work with discretion and maintain confidentiality

- Numerate and financially literate

- Flexible and adaptable, willing to go the extra mile

- A commitment to our ethos and values

## Corresponding interview questions for job description

*Opening questions*

- What do you know about Sierra Capital Investors and our work?

- What attracted you to this role?

- What interests you about working in Financial Services?

- Talk us through your CV to date and what you have learned from your career so far.

*Competency-based questions*

- Project Finance is a dynamic and challenging team at Sierra Capital Investors. Tell us about a time when you have worked in a pressurised environment. How did you feel about that experience, and how did you manage conflicting deadlines?

- Can you give us an example of a complex task you have worked on and how you ensured its success?

- Give us an example of when you delivered change to improve a process. How did you ensure its success?

- Please give an example of a time you had to deliver a message to a different audience. What did you do to ensure that it was understood and well received?

- Can you give us an example of a time you have worked with a difficult colleague and how you dealt with the situation?

*Character and interest questions*

- Why should we employ you? What sets you apart from other EAs? Give us an example of delivering a high standard of service.

- How would your current boss describe you?

- What aspect of this work do you find the most difficult/challenging, and why?

- If you were to be hired for this position, what would your first 100 days look like?

*Closing questions*

- Do you have any questions for us?

# Secret

After your interview, conduct a 'post-interview evaluation', a review of your interview. It is better to do this immediately after the interview, as soon as possible, whilst it is still fresh in your head. You might be reeling from the interview and not be in the mood, but it is a beneficial thing to do. You could do this on the train or bus on your way back from your face-to-face interview. You could use the notes facility on your smartphone.

If you were interviewed virtually, this is even easier. You can make notes immediately.

Note:
- Reflect on all the questions you were asked at the interview and how you responded.
- Think about your feelings about how it went.
- What could you have done better?

This reflection will help you to plan and prepare for your next interview. I call this 'interview experience'.

## Multiple interviews

You may have just one interview; however, having more than one interview for the role is not uncommon. At the beginning of the recruitment process, always ask how many interview stages you will have.

If you are called in for a second or subsequent stage of the interview process, that is promising. The interviewers have met with you, were impressed by your performance, and wish to learn more about you. It could also be because they would like you to meet with someone else whom you did not meet in the previous interview(s).

You should review your previous interview(s), as I advised before, and use this information to prepare. Use this opportunity to think about questions you thought about but forgot to ask. Do some more research based on the information you obtained from the interviewers. Remember that being called back is a good sign. Be confident and do your thing.

You can find examples of common interview questions in Appendix 6.

**Questions you should ask**

In the next chapter, I talk about job offers and acceptance. I mention how important it is to make the right decision when it's time to accept a job offer.

One of the ways you can ensure that you are making the right decision is to use the interview as your opportunity to ask questions that will help you find out whether this is indeed the right job and organisation for you.

That way, you minimise what I refer to as 'buyer's remorse' – regretting taking the job after you start.

There are no guarantees in life about anything. You can still accept a job and regret your decision, but asking the right questions will help you find out more and help you decide if you are offered the post.

Remember, the interview is a two-way process. You might be desperate for a job and worried about how this comes across, but any good employer will be happy to answer these questions. If they don't like you asking these types of questions, then you may wish to consider whether that organisation is the right one for you.

**Below are some pertinent questions you can ask:**

1. To whom will I be reporting?

2. What is the structure of the team?

3. How would you describe your team culture?

4. What do you like about working here?

5. Why is this position vacant?

6. Are the job responsibilities exactly as they are in the job description?

7. What are your immediate priorities?

8. How would you measure my performance?

9. What opportunities are there for my growth and my career progression?

10. What are your expectations around hybrid working?

11. How many days will I be expected to work from home or the office?

12. Tell me more about your recent launch/new product/merger/CEO.

13. What are the company's plans for the next 3/5 years?

*There is always something to be learned from every experience in life, good or bad.*

**Questions the interviewer should not ask you**

While I was writing this section, one of my mentees told me that, at a recent interview, she was asked how many sick days she had had in the last 12 months. Ironically, in that same interview, she was asked to name all the protected characteristics covered by the United Kingdom's (UK) Equality Act (https://www.legislation.gov.uk/ukpga/2010/15/section/4).

She responded to the question even though, as an HR professional, she knew that her interviewers should not be asking that question.

When you attend an interview and are desperate for a job, you might be compelled to answer questions you know you are not supposed to be asked in the first instance.
I will stress again that an interview is a two-way process, and no one has a right to make you feel uncomfortable or ask questions that could be deemed intrusive or illegal.

Asking a question about the number of sick days is inappropriate because you may have had numerous sick days as a result of an illness or a disability which is covered under the Equality Act. This rule applies to the UK, but many countries have similar legislation to protect employees, so if you are not in the UK, this is likely to apply to you too.

Legislation aside, this is not an ethical question to ask at an interview, so you may wish to consider whether you want to work for an employer who wants to ask this at an interview. A good response would be, 'My absence from work as a result of sickness did not hinder my performance in the past.'

You could be asked if you have a disability and whether you need any reasonable adjustments. This question is usually asked before the interview so they can make arrangements to support you. In that context, this is not a bad question.

Other questions you should not be asked at the interview include your age and marital status. If you are a woman, you should not be asked whether you are pregnant or expecting to be; you should not be asked your religion, or your sexual orientation.

You should also not be asked whether you have any criminal convictions. Criminal convictions will be disclosed as part of any screening process, and that is a separate conversation that should be held privately and with discretion.

**Note:**

Before the interview or after starting work, you may be asked to complete a Diversity and Inclusion questionnaire. That is simply for the employers' records and is used to implement and measure the effectiveness of Diversity and Inclusion policies. In this instance, it is up to you to complete this. However, as an HR professional committed to ensuring we have initiatives to support everyone, I would encourage you to complete it.

*Trust your gut.*
*It never lies.*

## Job offer and acceptance – How to avoid buyer's remorse

Job offers are usually made verbally and then followed up in writing.

Congratulations, you made it! You got the job!

You are now in a very strong position because they have gone through an entire recruitment process, and the company have now found their ideal candidate – YOU!

**I have a few secrets to share about this stage of the process.**

Employers also get nervous during the recruitment process. It costs time and money. The steps the hiring manager and recruitment team perform to secure a candidate include: designing the job description, advertising, using agencies, using executive search firms, putting the interview panel together, designing final questions, scoring the candidates, and the panel convening to make the final decision. All that is work!

So, they are also breathing a sigh of relief and hoping you will accept their offer. Accepting the offer is a life-changing moment. Ensuring that you accept the right role is important for your future.

If the job does not turn out to be what you thought it would be, or it doesn't meet your expectations, you will be dissatisfied and regret your decision, which means you may have to start job hunting again.

It is important to be focused and have clarity about what you want. When you have clarity about the job you want, you are less likely to be confused and accept a job that is not right for you.

To ensure that you make the right decision, check the terms of the offer and the contract. Don't just accept the job without checking the terms of the offer and the contract. Don't be afraid to ask questions if you are unsure about anything. Don't allow any agency or hiring manager to influence your decision.

Go with your gut. Trust your instincts.

**My personal experience**

In the past, I have been so excited at job offers that I impulsively accepted them on the spot. I have also allowed people to influence my decision. I have also been afraid to ask questions. However, when I started the job and realised it was not right for me, I had to deal with it alone. Now I take this step very seriously because having to start a job, realise it's not right, I didn't follow my instincts, and having to look again for another job was painful. In addition, it doesn't look good to stay somewhere for just a few months but having to stay in a job you don't like for a long time is not fun.

The terms of the offer will form the basis of your employment contract. Some employers send the contract with the offer letter at the same time.

Check the hours, check the salary, and check whether there is any clause you are concerned about before signing. Read the small print. Don't get carried away.

Now is the time to ask if they have hybrid working, whether you can work remotely from abroad for a few weeks a year, etc. Don't wait until you have started work.

**Dealing with multiple offers**

Another dilemma is what happens if you have more than one offer. Whilst this can seem like a good place to be, it can be stressful. I have been in that place many times.

I have learned that clarity over what you want and don't want will help you make the right decision. When considering multiple offers, it is worth noting that there is no perfect job, just like there is no perfect situation in life. There will always be trade-offs.

One way to help with the decision is to make a spreadsheet, highlighting the pros and cons of each job.

Consider what is important to you.

- Is it career progression?

- Is it money?

- Is it work-life balance?

Make a decision based on your immediate needs, but always consider the bigger picture.
For example, if it's a very low-paid job that will mean financial struggle, you may need to consider the implications. You will not be happy because of your financial struggles. However, if it doesn't pay well right now, you may be able to get by financially in the short term, and it offers career progression and long-term gains. Think about the bigger picture. Live within your means and be patient.

If you are still unsure, go back to your SWOT analysis and the results of the values and motivations questionnaires you have completed. Make a list of the pros and cons of each job and weigh these against your priorities and goals. Speak to your career coach if you have one. Remember that self-awareness and clarity are key to making the right decision.

# Preparing for your new job

Start getting your mind, body and soul ready for your new job.

Starting a new job, like any change, is an upheaval. You have to meet and get along with new people and learn about a new company, the company's culture, policies, ways of doing things, etc. You will need to get used to the journey, where everything is, etc. It is a change, and we all know that change can affect our equilibrium.

Be prepared. It is always advisable to take a break when you leave your current job before starting a new one.

You may have been unemployed for a while, applied for many jobs, and attended many interviews, so now you feel exhausted.

Take a few days off, recharge and refresh before starting your new job.

### The first 100 days

I am sure you know of the adage: 'First impressions count.'

Those first few days are key to your long-term success in the organisation.

Take your time to find out as much as possible during your induction period. Find out who the key people are, your team, etc.

Establish immediate priorities with your line manager and find out what you will be expected to deliver.

A good company will ensure you have a well-planned and well-structured induction. Research has shown that good induction is the key to increased engagement and productivity.

Finally, do not get involved in office politics. Be careful who you confide in, and trust no one. If you need to offload, speak to a loved one.

No job is easy. Nothing in life is easy, as you know.

All the best!

*Self-care is my superpower.*

# Self-care

# Avoiding job-hunting burnout

As an advocate of health and well-being, it would be remiss of me if I did not mention the importance of taking good care of yourself whilst job hunting.

It is indeed an anxious and stressful process for most people, especially those under pressure financially. I have alluded to this in other sections of the book when I advised caution against coming across as desperate during interviews because you need to earn. That said, it is perfectly understandable when under pressure.

Therefore, it is very important to make your well-being a priority. You are likely to perform better at interviews and secure the job you want if you are healthy and of sound mind. Think about your health too. A positive mind is key to healthy living. Do not encourage negative vibes.

**Some suggestions are below:**

- Don't apply for jobs in a panic. Slow down and apply only for jobs of interest to you.
- Develop a realistic schedule. Don't spend all your waking hours applying for jobs. Have a schedule and plan your time effectively. For example, you can work two hours in the

morning to complete job applications, tailoring your CV for each role. You can schedule another couple of hours to update your skills or read up on relevant information tailored to your job search.

- Network with helpful people. Find a trusted recruiter who has your back.
- Always ensure you get some rest before and after your interviews.
- Call up a friend or someone who makes you laugh.
- Eat your favourite meal.
- Don't take rejections personally.
- Exercise.
- Express gratitude.
- Go for a walk.
- Listen to music.
- Pray, meditate or both.
- Relax and spend time with your loved ones.
- Seek help if it's getting too much and you feel you can't cope.
- Show some kindness.
- Take a relaxing bath.
- Watch a funny movie.

# Epilogue

I wrote this book to help you to secure your dream job. I have experienced all the highs and lows of the job-hunting process so I know what it feels like.

I have been through numerous job applications, experienced rejections, recruiters not getting back to me, regrets when I felt like I had made the wrong choice; at the same time, I have managed to secure dream jobs with leading global companies. I see past failures as lessons learned.

As a HR and recruitment professional, I see the process from the other side too because I am there from the beginning when the business wants to grow and hire new people. I design the business structure, the job description, the advert and the interview questions. I participate in the hiring process so I know what a good candidate looks like.

Everything I have shared in my book is based on my personal and professional experience. I have written from the heart, providing you with practical help and advice for the job-hunting journey.
I had to learn the hard way, I did not have anyone to tell me about the myths, secrets and truths I have shared with you. Some of the mistakes I made on my journey were disappointing and painful, so I wouldn't want people to experience them.

I am confident, therefore, that if you follow my advice, my hints and tips, and use my quotes when the going gets tough, you will achieve your goal.

With all good wishes for your future success.

Warmest regards

Willorna

*Baby steps.*
*Be proud of each step*
*you take towards*
*reaching your goal.*

# About the Author

Willorna Brock is an experienced Human Resources professional and coach. Willorna is an expert in all aspects of the recruitment process, from helping managers design their teams and the roles they need, drafting the job descriptions and adverts, to shortlisting and interview selection for candidates at all levels. She has also worked in graduate recruitment and induction.

From her very first (Saturday) job on a market stall at age 14, she has worked for some of the world's leading organisations, including Atkins, CGI, EY, HSBC, NatWest, PWC and Société Générale.

As a former teacher, Willorna is passionate about helping people to do well and fulfil their potential.
She has been coaching and mentoring for over 20 years and has a proven track record of enabling people to secure their dream jobs.

She founded her own HR Advisory and Career-Coaching business – Goshenn HR – providing HR advice to small and medium-sized businesses (SMEs), and career, executive and personal coaching to individuals.

Willorna is also passionate about mental health and well-being, with her mantra 'living life fullest'. She regularly writes about this on her social media platform 'The No Drama Lounge'.

## Services

Goshenn HR is for small-medium enterprises and individuals who want a working culture that fundamentally values the holistic well-being and professional development of people, which is the foundation for overall business success.

My company's mission is to **empower a culture of well-being and person-centred development in the world of work.**

My company's vision is **harmony and wholeness** for business and people.

I talk about humans, not processes; my frames of reference are real human experiences (real lives, real people).

I offer holistic coaching to ensure that businesses and people can benefit from **integrated** HR process development and training services.

**HR Services**

Human Resources Advisory for Small and Medium-Sized Enterprises (SMEs)

- Start-ups looking to employ people for the first time
- Growing companies experiencing rapid scaling in their business
- Established SMEs who want to change/improve their company culture
- Managers and team leaders who are accountable for managing people and need support with people management

**Coaching**

- Career coaching – job-seeking individuals who require coaching to find employment aligned with their values

- Executive and personal coaching – helping people find meaning and purpose in their lives, making the best use of their talents

**Courses**

- Online job-hunting courses
- Career masterclasses – online and in-person

# Useful links

- www.nationalcareers.service.gov.uk
- https://www.careermetis.com/top-10-skills-for-the-successful-21st-century-worker/
- https://www.jobscan.co
- https://www.skillsyouneed.com/rhubarb/job-market-value.html
- https://www.weforum.org/agenda/2016/01/the-10-skills-you-need-to-thrive-in-the-fourth-industrial-revolution/
- www.prospects.ac.uk
- www.resume.io

# Appendices

## Appendix 1:
## Example CV

Jane Smith
Address Town, Postcode
Email Tel no

PROFILE

SKILLS

EDUCATION

WORK EXPERIENCE

Provide details of each employer, job title and dates as below:

Date from – Date to
Name of Employer
Job Title

Give a short paragraph with a brief outline of your role, followed by bullet points describing your responsibilities. (Three to four bullets are fine.) Remember to highlight achievements, the value you added, the difference you made, or the problem you solved. It is important to use quantifiers or data to demonstrate impact.

For example:

- Introduced a new financial accounting package which led to a 50% reduction in errors in 12 months
- Devised and launched an investment strategy, increasing profits by £500K in one year
- Successfully resolved a complex case, leading to improved team morale

AWARDS/VOLUNTARY WORK

INTERESTS

## Appendix 2:
## Example cover letter

Address
Date

Company name
Company address

Dear Sir/Madam/Recruitment Manager/Named person
Re: Job title
Paragraph 1

Introduction. Why you are writing? Where you saw the job advertised.

*Example*: Thank you for the opportunity to submit my application for the above position, which I saw advertised on XXX.
Please find attached a copy of my CV.

Paragraph 2

Why you are suitable for the job. Talk about your skills and achievements in relation to the job description and how this would add value to the employer. Why they should employ you. The paragraph needs to be brief and not regurgitate your CV.

*Example:* As you can see from my attached CV, I am experienced in XXX and have done XXX.

Paragraph 3

Show your knowledge and interest in the company. Talk about what you know about them and why you want to work for them. Discuss how you would fit in and help their success.

*Example:* I have always been interested in working for XXX. Your ethos and values match my own, and I believe I bring XXX, which will add value.

Final paragraph

Finish with a roundup and mention that you are looking forward to the interview.

*Example:* I am firmly committed to my career and personal development and try to keep up to date with developments in XXX. I am eager to demonstrate my abilities during the interview process and look forward to an opportunity to discuss your needs in further detail. Thank you for your time and consideration.

Yours faithfully/sincerely,*

XXX(* - 'sincerely' if you're writing to a named individual; 'faithfully' if you're writing to 'Sir/Madam' or job title)

## Appendix 3:
## Example of speculative email

In the opening paragraph, explain what sort of role you're looking for. Then, show you've done your research by explaining why you're attracted to the company. Next, you need to talk about the skills and experience you have gained relevant to the company and the type of role you seek. It's best to show that you're an all-rounder, so don't restrict yourself by focusing on one skill or area. Finally, you should end on a positive note.

Use the format below:

1. Introduction
2. Explain what role you are looking for
3. Talk about your research into the company and why you are attracted to the company
4. Talk about your skills and experience which are relevant to the job and the company
5. End on a positive note, saying you are looking forward to hearing from them

Example (when you don't know them)

Dear XXX

Hope you don't mind my direct approach.

I have been following your company, and I am attracted to XXX.

I have a wide range of XXX experience, having worked at XXX.

I attach a copy of my CV and would relish a chance to discuss possible openings at XXX.

Thank you in advance for taking the time to review my CV.

I look forward to hearing from you in due course.

Warm regards

Yours sincerely

XXX

Example (when someone has referred you)

Dear XXX

I trust this email finds you well.

My friend and ex-colleague XXX gave me your contact details as I am seeking my next Marketing Executive opportunity.

I have a wide range of marketing experience, having worked in contract roles in various, mostly global, organisations in the public, private and not-for-profit sectors. I am now looking for an opportunity in a commercial organisation where I can add value.

I attach a copy of my CV and would relish a chance to discuss possible openings at XXX.

Thank you in advance for taking the time to review my CV. Looking forward to hearing from you in due course.

Warm regards

Yours sincerely
XXX

## Appendix 4:
## Additional interview questions

It is a good idea to prepare for some of the below questions.

- Tell me about yourself.

- How do you handle conflict?

- How do you add value?

- How do you react to criticism?

- How do you react to pressurised situations?

- How resilient are you?

- How would your current boss describe you?

- How would your work colleagues describe you?

- What accomplishments are you most proud of, and why?

- What are your career aspirations?

- What do you personally bring to a team?

- What drives you?

- What frustrations did you encounter in your last job, and how did you overcome them?
- What is your leadership style?
- What qualities make you a good leader?
- What role do you take within group projects?
- What specifically about this role will motivate you?
- What strategies or methods do you use to de-stress?
- What are your salary expectations?
- Where do you want to be in 5 years?
- Why should we hire you?
- Tell me about a time you had to learn something quickly.
- Tell me about a time you failed or made a mistake. What did you learn from it?
- Tell me about a time you had to work with a difficult person.

- Tell me about a time you had to persuade someone to see your point of view.
- Tell me about a time you had to manage conflicting priorities.

## Appendix 5:
## Career coaching case studies

I have compiled three sets of questions from previous coaching clients, and below, you can see my advice to them. Everyone I have helped has managed to secure a job. Please note that names have been changed to maintain anonymity and confidentiality.

1.  Question from a 23-year-old recent business and management graduate, seeking a job in a commercial organisation, preferably in the City of London.

*I have been struggling to get a full-time job because I don't have much office-based work experience. I have had weekend and holiday jobs, mostly in retail and hospitality. I have a part-time job as a Customer Service Associate in the hospitality industry, a role I have had since I was 18. I need help with putting my CV together. I am not confident because I am the first in my family to attend university.*

My advice

I met Ben for an initial coaching session where I tried to boost his confidence and encouraged him to kick-start his career.

I asked Ben to consider his strengths, weaknesses, passions, and motivation. We carried out some research into possible career choices. I asked him to narrow his choices and decide exactly what he wanted to do. Wanting to work in a 'commercial organisation' is too broad. He needed to list three possible careers. During our conversations, we developed a CV from the SWOT analysis. Ben realised he already possessed valuable skills from his university course and work experience.

Armed with a new CV and interview coaching, Ben developed renewed confidence. On my advice, he approached his current employer for job shadowing in their sales and marketing department. After a couple of months, Ben was offered a role as a Marketing Assistant.

Lessons learned

Don't underestimate your skills and abilities. As a new graduate, it is valuable if you already have work experience, even if it's not in the field you wish to work in. If you have a part-time or a holiday job, even better. You have nothing to lose but a lot to gain by asking if you can apply for a role in the area you want or even engage in job shadowing or work experience.

All good employers reward loyalty and will be keen to develop their staff. A lot of CEOs started in junior roles. For example, Ursula Burns started as an intern at Xerox in 1980 and was named CEO in 2009.

2. Question from a 32-year-old single mum of one, seeking a role that will allow her to go up the career ladder and juggle her responsibilities as a mother.

*I am an English graduate with a Master's in Business Management. I have a daughter who is just about to start school. I have been struggling to find a full-time job because all the jobs I have been applying for do not offer flexible work. I need to be able to collect my daughter from school some days and have some flexibility during the holidays. I have been doing quite a lot on the side – I am quite creative and like writing, so I have been vlogging on YouTube about lifestyle and setting up a local Mums' network.*

*I need help with my CV, and I need help with my job search. In previous interviews, I struggled with knowing the right questions. I also want to find out about my rights at work.*

My advice

Mary was asked to complete my career-coaching questionnaire, requesting candidates to complete their SWOT analysis before our initial meeting. Mary also completed a psychometric test for self-analysis to determine her strengths and how she works best.

Before embarking on any job search, as I mentioned earlier, it is essential to know what you would like to do. Set your goals. Ask yourself, 'In an ideal world, what would I like to do?' Mary had been too focused on her single mum status. Whilst this is worth considering because we need to be realistic about the choices we make at various stages of our lives, it is always best to start with your ideal goal in mind. After that, you can work out what you need to do to achieve it.

Mary's strengths were in communications, evident from her vlogging and setting up the mums' group. She discovered she would enjoy a role in communication and engagement within a business.

We had to consider roles that would give some flexibility. After working on Mary's CV, I advised her to start exploring job sites that targeted parents, such as workingmums.co.uk, and to research companies that have been applauded for championing diversity and supporting working parents.

I provided interview preparation support, including establishing whether the employer would be open to flexible working, when to ask the question, etc.

Mary finally secured a role with a leading employer as a Communications Officer. She can work from home twice a week during term-time and three days a week during the school holidays. As a lot of communications work can be done remotely, this was the ideal career choice for Mary, given her qualifications and circumstances.

Lessons learned

When faced with uncertainty over your career choice, be honest and conduct some self-analysis as a starting point. The career SWOT analysis is a good starting point. Use your end goal as a target. That will enable you to focus and strategize.

Don't allow your present circumstances to get in the way of your goals. Remember, nothing lasts forever. If you are a parent with young children, they will not be small forever. Time flies. Don't allow that to limit your choices. Plan and think of the bigger picture.

3. Question from a 17-year-old sixth-former looking for a weekend job.

*I have just started Sixth Form, studying 'A' levels and hoping to attend university. I love fashion and always follow and write about fashion trends on Instagram. I have never done any work before, and I don't know how to write a CV. I did the Duke of Edinburgh Award and The Challenge during school and participated in many activities.*

My advice

Sarah was given some advice on doing her first CV. When doing her CV, Sarah realised she had transferable skills from being the eldest in her family, babysitting and extra-curricular activities, which are valuable to an employer.

Sarah decided she loved fashion and would find a weekend job in a fashion store. I advised Sarah to go into stores and build a rapport with the staff to ask whether they had any vacancies. That would yield better results than trying to apply for jobs online.

Sarah went into an H&M store, got along quite well with the manager, and was invited to attend an interview.

I provided interview coaching, and Sarah secured her first weekend job.

Lessons learned

Young people who do not have work experience have to start somewhere. It is important to try and engage in extra-curricular activities in school, such as sports, drama, being a mentor to a younger pupil, and being a class representative – all transferable skills you can sell to an employer.

There are plenty of links online to help you.

Printed in Great Britain
by Amazon